D1275877

Feb 13, 1989

Jane,

May your house be cat-filled
and your litter box be oder-free.

Thanks;

Leo

CAT
snaps

MARTIN LEMAN'S
CAT
snaps

PELHAM BOOKS

For cats & cat lovers

PELHAM BOOKS

Published by the Penguin Group
27 Wrights Lane, London W8 5TZ, England
Viking Penguin Inc., 40 West 23rd Street, New York, New York 10010, USA
Penguin Books Australia Ltd, Ringwood, Victoria, Australia
Penguin Books Canada Ltd, 2801 John Street, Markham, Ontario, Canada L3R 1B4
Penguin Books (NZ) Ltd, 182-190 Wairau Road, Auckland 10, New Zealand

Penguin Books Ltd, Registered Offices: Harmondsworth, Middlesex, England

Research and design by Jill Leman
First published in 1987
Reprinted 1988

Copyright © Jill and Martin Leman 1987

British Library Cataloguing in Publication Data

Leman, Jill
Catsnaps.
1. Cats – Poetry
I. Title   II. Leman, Martin
636.8   SF445.5

ISBN 0-7207-1731-0

Printed by New Interlitho, Milan

Oh cat; I'd say, or pray: be-ooootiful cat!
Delicious cat! Exquisite cat! Satiny cat!
Cat like a soft owl, cat with paws like moths;
jewelled cat, miraculous cat!
Cat, cat, cat, cat.

Doris Lessing

Black and white cats wear evening dress so elegantly

Some cats, as we all know, are born in full evening dress. White shirt, white tie ... (whiskers) ... black tails and all. The illusion is perfect, particularly when they also have smart black paws to match. I love cats in evening dress; they wear it so much more elegantly than we do. Moreover they never look incongruous in it.

Beverley Nichols

Deep in cat's eyes lies the sheen of a butterfly's wing

*I*n grey cat's eyes lay the green sheen of a jade butterfly's wing, as if an artist had said: what could be as graceful, as delicate as a cat? What more naturally the creature of the air? What air-being has affinity with cat? Butterfly, butterfly of course! And there, deep in cat's eyes lies this thought, hinted at merely, with a half laugh; and hidden behind the fringes of lashes, behind the fine brown inner lid, and the evasions of cat-coquetry.

Doris Lessing

A cat-owner's thoughts on the meaning of life

I have two cat-doors in my own house; one of them leads from the kitchen down a flight of steps into a little courtyard; the other leads straight from the music-room on to the open lawn. The gentle sound of the doors swinging backwards and forwards at all times of the day and the night, is a pleasing accompaniment to my life; it reminds me that the cats are alert and fully occupied and intent upon their many tasks of inspection, espionage and sentry work. Often, when I have been feeling lonely, when a book has been thrust aside in boredom, when the keys of the piano, softly lit, hold no invitation to the dance, I have lain back and stared at the shadows on the ceiling, wondering what life is all about . . . and then, suddenly, there is the echo of the swinging door, and across the carpet, walking with the utmost delicacy and precision, stalks 'Four' or 'Five' or Oscar. Whichever it may be, his tail is always very upright, and as he walks he talks . . . small, friendly, feline talk, delivered in the softest of mews . . . mews which melt into purrs as he approaches the sofa. He sits down on the floor beside me, regarding my long legs, my old jumper, and my floppy arms, with a purely practical interest. Which part of this large male body will form the most appropriate lap? Usually he settles for the chest. Whereupon he springs up and there is a feeling of cold fur – for the night is frosty – and the tip of an icy nose, thrust against my wrist and a positive tattoo of purrs. And I no longer wonder what life is all about.

Beverley Nichols

Cat-ideas and mouse-ideas

We can never get rid of mouse-ideas completely, they keep turning up again and again, and nibble, nibble – no matter how often we drive them off. The best way to keep them down is to have a few good strong cat-ideas which will embrace them and ensure their not reappearing till they do so in another shape.

Samuel Butler

Mrs Dilke's cats

*M*rs Dilke has two Cats – a Mother and a Daughter – now the Mother is a tabby and the daughter a black and white like the spotted child – Now it appears quite ominous to me, for the doors of both houses are opened frequently – so that there is a complete thoroughfare for both Cats (there being no board up to the contrary) they may one and several of them come into my room *ad libitum*. But no – the Tabby only comes – whether from sympathy from Ann the Maid or me I can not tell ... The Cat is not an old Maid herself – her daughter is a proof of it – I have questioned her – I have look'd at the lines of her paw – I have felt her pulse – to no purpose. Why should the *old* Cat come to me? I ask myself – and myself has not a word to answer.

John Keats

An affectionate interest in the naming of cats

*I*t occurs to me as I write this that the naming of cats is an almost infallible guide to the degree of affection bestowed on a cat. Perhaps not affection so much as true appreciation of feline character. You may be reasonably sure when you meet a cat called Ginger or Nigger or merely Puss that his or her owner has insufficient respect for his cat. Such plebeian and unimaginative names are not given to cats by true cat lovers. There is a world of difference between the commonplace 'Tibby' and the dignified and sonorous 'Tabitha Longclaws Tiddleywinks' which the poet Hood christened his cat. And her three kittens called Pepperpot, Scratchaway and Sootikins reveal an affectionate interest which is never displayed by such ordinary names as Sandy or Micky . . .

Not that grandiloquent or fancy titles are necessary to a true appreciation of cats. What could be more dignified or appropriate than the name of Doctor Johnson's cat Hodge? . . .

Without doubt the names given to individual cats shed interesting light on their human owners. No one but a true cat lover could call his cat Gilderoy, Absalom, Potiphar, Wotan, Feathers or Shah de Perse.

It may be thought that such elegant names are difficult to live up to, and it is true that in ordinary usage even the most fervent cat lover will use a convenient abbreviation. But I am sure every true lover of cats will agree that there are times when nothing less than full ceremonial titles will serve.

Michael Joseph

Extract from Miss Topping's will, Vendôme, May 1841

*I*desire that there shall be raised from the most easily convertible part of my property a capital sum sufficient to produce 800f. a year, which shall be paid quarterly to such person as I may name ... on condition of taking the care and nourishment of my three favourite cats, Nina, Fanfan and Mini ... The person (so) appointed shall live on a ground floor, to which shall adjoin a terrace easy of access and a garden enclosed within walls, of which they shall have full and free enjoyment ... They are to sleep in the house, and therefore are to be shut up after their supper.

A *scene of domestic harmony*

A blazing fire, a warm rug, candles lit and curtains drawn, the kettle on for tea, and finally the cat before you, attracting your attention – it is a scene which everybody likes. The cat purrs, as if it applauded our consideration, and gently moves its tail ... Now she proceeds to clean herself all over ... beginning with her paws, and fetching amazing tongues at her hind-hips. Anon, she scratches her neck with a foot of rapid delight, leaning her head towards it, and shuttering her eyes half to accommodate the action of the skin and half to enjoy the luxury. She then rewards her paws with a few more touches – look at the action of her head and neck, how pleasing it is, the ears pointed forward, and the neck gently arching to and fro. Finally she gives a sneeze, and another twist of mouth and whiskers, and then, curling her tail towards her front claws, settles herself on her hind quarters in an attitude of bland meditation ...

Leigh Hunt

Poised on silvery paws

*H*er two creamy lightly barred front legs were straight down side by side, on two silvery paws. Her ears, lightly fringed with white that looked silver, lifted and moved, back, forward, listening and sensing. Her face turned, slightly, after each new sensation, alert. Her tail moved, in another dimension, as if its tip was catching messages her other organs could not. She sat poised, air-light, looking, hearing, feeling, smelling, breathing, with all of her, fur, whiskers, ears – everything, in delicate vibration. If a fish is the movement of water embodied, given shape, then cat is a diagram and pattern of subtle air.

Doris Lessing

Cats and flowers

*C*ats and flowers have played so large a part in my life that I can scarcely think of one without the other. In a cluster of wild hyacinths I can see reflected the blue eyes of my first Siamese; on warm May mornings he would wander to the shadow of an old wall where the hyacinths had come by chance, and dispose himself most elegantly upon them. If reproached for squashing the hyacinths, he merely blinked; the blue eyes and the blue flowers, mingling together, were so beautiful that there was nothing to be done about it.

Beverley Nichols

Don Pierrot of Navarre

*D*on Pierrot of Navarre always sat up at night until I came home, waiting for me on the inside of the door, and as soon as I stepped into the antechamber he would come rubbing himself against my legs, arching his back and purring in gladsome, friendly fashion. Then he would start to walk in front of me, preceding me like a page, and I am sure that if I had asked him to do so, he would have carried my candle. In this way he would escort me to my bedroom, wait until I had undressed, jump up on the bed, put his paws round my neck, rub his nose against mine, lick me with his tiny red tongue, rough as a file, and utter little inarticulate cries by way of expressing unmistakably the pleasure he felt at seeing me again. When he had sufficiently caressed me and it was time to sleep, he used to perch upon the backboard of his bed and slept there like a bird roosting on a branch. As soon as I woke in the morning, he would come and stretch out beside me until I rose.

Théophile Gautier

Edward Lear and Foss

When staying at Cannes at Christmas, 1882, I was invited by Mr Lear to go over to San Remo to spend a few days with him. Mr Lear's villa was large, and the second he had built; the first became unbearable to him from a large hotel having been planted in front of it. So he put his new house in a place by the sea, where, as he said, nothing could interrupt his light unless the fishes built. The second house was exactly like the first. This, Mr Lear explained to me, was necessary or else Foss, his cat, might not have approved of the new villa.

from a letter written by Henry Strachey

A very fine cat indeed

I shall never forget the indulgence with which he treated Hodge, his cat; for whom he himself used to go out and buy oysters, lest the servants having that trouble should take a dislike to the poor creature. I am, unluckily, one of those who have an antipathy to a cat, so that I am uneasy when in the room with one; and I own, I frequently suffered a good deal from the presence of this same Hodge. I recollect him one day scrambling up Dr Johnson's breast, apparently with much satisfaction, while my friend, smiling and half-whistling, rubbed down his back, and pulled him by the tail; and when I observed he was a fine cat, saying, 'Why, yes, Sir, but I have had cats whom I liked better than this;' and then, as if perceiving Hodge to be out of countenance, adding, 'but he is a very fine cat, a very fine cat indeed.'

from James Boswell's Life of Johnson

Ailurophobe and ailurophile

A person who actually does not like cats is called an ailurophobe, and will quite likely go to his tomb without ever knowing that Turkish cats like swimming, that blue-eyed whites are usually deaf, that when the Earl of Southampton was imprisoned in the Tower his cat came down the chimney to him, that a cat called 'Pussycat' fell 120 feet from a block of flats in Maida Vale on March 7th 1965 and landed unhurt, that 100,000 cats are employed by the British Civil Service, that 'tabby' was the name for a striped silk made in Attabiy, a quarter of Baghdad named after Attab, son of Omeyya, and that is why striped cats are called tabbies.

A cat-lover, or ailurophile, would of course prefer to think that the striped silk was named after the cat, and that Tibshelf, a village in Derbyshire, is a natural rock shelf lined with huge cats like those still seen on the window-sills of St Ives, in the houses which have window-sills large enough. This is unfortunately not true. However, it is a simple matter to call the shelf on which your cats like to sleep, high up out of the reach of people, when it is too wet to scrabble up 60-foot trees, the tibshelf.

Even in households where an ailurophobe is married to an ailurophile it is fairly likely that there will be more than one cat. It is very hard to have just one cat. This is not only because it is perfectly possible for you to have a kitten who starts peering in all your cupboards after you have had her for ten days, looking for places to have the kittens that she is already carrying, and will shortly have with the utmost nonchalance, leaving absolutely no mess, just these three slightly smaller kittens, before you have even begun to think about 'taking her to the vet' as ailurophiles put it. You may, for instance, have a tom who was taken to the vet years ago, and now looks like Osmin, the enormous guardian of the harem in Mozart's opera Il Seraglio. 'He is getting old,' you will find yourself saying (even if you are the ailurophobe), 'it will be awful when he dies, let's get another one and sort of play it in.'

Paul Jennings

Green, green eyes; but in shadow, a dark smoky gold

*O*r, deliberate, she would crouch and fascinate me with her eyes. I stared into them, almond-shaped in their fine outline of dark pencil, around which was a second pencilling of cream. Under each, a brush stroke of dark. Green, green eyes; but in shadow, a dark smoky gold – a dark-eyed cat. But in the light, green, a clear cool emerald. Behind the transparent globes of the eyeball, slices of veined gleaming butterfly wing. Wings like jewels – the essence of wing.

Doris Lessing

An affectionate start to the day

I have just been called to the door by the sweet voice of Tossa, whose morning proceedings are wonderful – she has just jumped on my lap, and her beautiful tail has made this smudge. I was going to say that she sleeps on an armchair before the drawing room fire and enters Flu's room with Eliza regularly at half past seven. Then she comes to my room and gives a mew: and then, especially if I let her in and go on writing without taking notice of her, there is a real demonstration of affection for five minutes such as never again occurs in the day. She purrs, she walks round and round me. She jumps on my lap, she turns to me and rubs her head and nose against my chin: she opens her mouth and raps her pretty white teeth against my pen: then she jumps down, settles herself before the fire, and never shows any more affection that day.

Matthew Arnold

Memories of Calvin

We understood each other perfectly, but we never made any fuss about it; when I spoke his name and snapped my fingers, he came to me; when I returned home at night, he was pretty sure to be waiting for me near the gate, and would rise and saunter along the walk, as if his being there was purely accidental – so shy was he commonly of showing feeling. There was one thing he never did – he never rushed through an open doorway. He never forgot his dignity. If he had asked to have the door opened, and was eager to go out, he always went out deliberately; I can see him now, standing on the sill, looking about at the sky as if he was thinking whether it was worthwhile to take an umbrella, until he was near having his tail shut in.

Charles Dudley Warner

Acknowledgements

We would like to thank the following for permission to use extracts:
Michael Joseph Ltd for *Particularly Cats* by Doris Lessing
and *A Dictionary of Cat Lovers* by Christabel Aberconway.
Jonathan Cape Ltd for *Cats ABC and XYZ* by Beverley Nichols.
Hugh Joseph for *Charles: the story of a friendship* by Michael Joseph.
Paul Jennings for 'Ailurophobe and Ailurophile'.
Rosalie Mander for *CAT-egories*, published by Weidenfeld and Nicolson Ltd.

The editor and publishers apologise for any omissions
and would be pleased to hear from those
whom they were unable to trace.

We should also like to thank all the owners of the cats
whose photographs are in this book,
especially those from London and St Ives, Cornwall.